Empowered
(The Dawning Of A New Day)

Acknowledgments

Cover Design
Robin Johnson
RL Design
386-338-3888
PO Box 19971
Jacksonville, FL, 32245
Https://gobookcoverdesign.com
robin@gobookcoverdesign.com

Copyright

ISBN: 9781707175000

ASIN: 1707175004

CHAPTERS

Preface   6

1.   Metamorphosis   14

2.   Empowered   24

3.   It Is Not money you need – It Is favour   44

4.   The Dawning Of A New Day   55

5.   Living Outside The Bubble   63

6.   In Whom Do You Trust?   74

7.   What Is In Your Hand?   85

8.   What You See Is What You Get   97

Bibliography   105

PREFACE

The Bible is the one book that has had, and continues to have, the greatest impact on nations throughout the world in terms of our belief systems, literature, history, and culture. Those nations who have embraced the teachings of the Bible have experienced prosperity, wisdom, and clarity of thinking, in making strategic decisions specifically in relation to their economy, political framework, and society generally.

My hope is that the reader will have the opportunity to experience the empowering teachings of the gospel and to impart what I believe, is the truth to one's quest in understanding one's purpose in life; that the meaning of life starts and ends with the Bible. Through the teachings of the Bible, we can become empowered to live out our God-given purpose and destiny so that we are empowered to prosper, to make a difference in our own communities, in our respective worlds, and to be positioned to leave a legacy for generations to come. Prosperity is not solely about becoming wealthy in monetary terms but also means we are equipped to progress forward in the way we live and how others are enabled to live too! Be-coming empowered means we are positioned to prosper, to make an impact on our communities, so that we can provide counsel to governments and political bodies alike, and to be positioned to exert Godly leverage to the leaders of our nations and political systems. Moreover, when we become empowered, we are better equipped to train our children to become the leaders of tomorrow. For me, the word be-come or be-coming, speaks of beginning to be like, live like and behave like, prosperous purpose-centered individuals.

The scriptures speak of God be-coming our salvation. In this regard, note specifically the scriptures in Psalm 118:14,21, and Isaiah 12:2. We shall look at these scriptures in detail later in the book.

Everyone is born for a God-given purpose and empowered by DNA (unique to the individual concerned), which equips the individual with the potential to live out that purpose. There is nothing new under the sun. Therefore, whatever is and will be in the scheme of the plan of God for our lives, is attainable and accessible to all that will thirst and seek after it; but first, we need to link with purpose.

It is imperative that we make that all-important connection with purpose, through reconciling with the author and the creator and Lord of our lives, Jesus Christ. By doing so we are positioned and postured to receive that same creative ability and enabling power which our father desires to impart to us, when we become His sons and daughters. When we reconcile with God, we are effectively saying that we receive His plan for salvation (i.e., reconciliation, restoration, and empowerment). We also receive his love for us and boldly making the statement that we accept that God sent his Son Jesus to die for our sins, that we through Him might have life. As a believer we then be-come equipped to live an abundant prosperous life through Jesus Christ and be equipped, to empower others, influence others for God, take territories, and have dominion on the earth.

Someone somewhere, is waiting on you to make that all-important connection and discover your purpose.

Ever more so in this changing economic climate, it is imperative that people are inspired and encouraged to find true purpose and the meaning of life.

Jesus, begotten of the Father who loves and cares so much for us, made the ultimate sacrifice when he died at the cross at Calvary, that we might have the best that heaven can afford us. It was not a selfish love but the demonstration of agape love which is unconditional and knows no limits. A love that is blind to colour creed and nationality. A love that shines on everyone irrespective of their start in life. A love that starts everyone at equal and equips us with the potential and grace to succeed in life; this potential being partly based on our ability to tap into the supernatural power of God and see what he sees and embrace the creative power that emanates only from him.

For those of us who feel that their case is hopeless because life has dealt harshly with you, note there is hope. Know that your adverse experiences are aimed at empowering you and can act as steppingstones to build the future that you desire. Also know that without a challenge, there will be no change. You need to challenge that situation, experience, problem, that has threatened to hold progress back. You can challenge that situation with the word of God and establish and surround yourself with a network of people who support your vision. Most of all, you must be your main motivator and remain focused and determined to succeed!

This book presents the truth of the gospel in a practical manner and can be used as a study guide by believers and non-believers alike, providing clarity on how to live empowered lives and offering counsel advice wisdom and practical solutions for everyday situations.

The book also issues a challenge to the Church, that we should be about empowering people to live abundant lives and empowering people for service. People need to be taught how to initiate progress by making the necessary steps to bring about change. People also need to be taught how to apply the word of God in their lives so that they can make progress. Moreover, the role of the church should be to empower God's people to reign, to take dominion over their lives, and exercise authority by the word of God, over problematic situations.

It is only by returning to God's original plan for humanity, that we can exercise authority and effective leadership and apply Godly wisdom to the myriad of situations we may face.

In particular, the problems facing our disenfranchised youth today.

Chapter 1

METAMORPHOSIS

Metamorphism charts the process from infancy to adulthood. It is indeed a necessary process of transition. Take for example the life of an insect, say the caterpillar, and its transition or metamorphosis into a butterfly. The larva is unlike the adult at its birth. Generally, the larva is in the feeding and growing stage, eating voraciously, shedding its cuticle several times, and growing rapidly. When it has reached full size, the larva becomes inactive, neither moving nor feeding, and extensive breakdown and reorganization takes place within the body, as eventually, a new life is formed. We can draw parallels from this process of transition when as believers we follow through the stages of training for destiny from preparation to process, and from process, (i.e., the making of one), to the manifestation, and the unveiling of the new person as we step into mature believers and become empowered to live out our purpose.

Breakdown of the 'old' nature occurs because God is continuing to replace the old life and its systems, ideals, and mind-sets, with the new agenda and the plans he has for us in our purpose. 'For God knows the thoughts he has for us; thoughts of good and not of evil, to give us an expected end.' (Jeremiah 29:11) God is not interested in the lack lustre routine that we can so often embrace, but rather he desires to see us fulfill our potential.

In examining the scenario, let us consider for one moment, being in a job which routinely brings in a psaltery sum every week sufficient to pay the bills, keeps a roof over our heads, puts food on the table, but offers little stimulus in the way of challenge and promotion. It only takes the rumble of the threat of redundancy, and/or company relocation, to get us thinking of other possibilities and 'taking stock' of where we are now - what do we really want to do? Up to this point we were prepared to 'join the rat race' for little gain and live below our potential worth. Furthermore, things we are used to doing and which have up until now formed an integral part of our life, start to breakdown or close. It is at this time, that we begin to discover new talents and skills which have laid dormant, but which have a license now to surface. Throughout this time extensive changes are taking place, and because of this process, transition can be a difficult time because very often, we would rather stick with that which we know than venture into a world that is relatively new and unknown.

Back to the caterpillar who is now nearing the end of its shelf life.................................

The caterpillar is constantly shedding its skin, and by rhythmic contractions of the body it pushes off the old cuticle and makes way for the new. What emerges is called the pupa. From the appearance of the pupa, and before the final molt, extensive changes have taken place; the outline of the adult's legs, proboscis eyes and wings, can be seen in its cuticle. Likewise, somewhere in the process of transition it becomes apparent where God is taking us, as the bits of the jigsaw begin to make sense and come together to form the true image of who we really are in Him.

In our process years, we are constantly shelving old habits, 'die hard,' old mind sets, to make way for the new being. The rhythmic contractions of a caterpillar mirror that of the process of birthing when at the time of labour. As the caterpillar comes to the end of this period, the pupa skin splits down the back and the adult insect pulls itself out of the skin and a beautiful butterfly is born. The caterpillar be-comes that beautiful butterfly and a new life begins in earnest.

The Process Of Be-coming

The process from caterpillar to butterfly takes 7-10 days. The number 7 symbolizes completion. If we look at biblical principles, we can see that the process of creation took 6 days and that God rested on the seventh day: this being the day of completion. In fact, the Bible says he rested from all his works on the seventh day in the knowledge that his mission had been completed or accomplished. Note in the scripture of Genesis Chapter 1:13, that in three days the foundations to the earth were being laid and were beginning to take shape. Similarly, it is interesting to note that butterflies emerge from the chrysalides in 7-10 days, but their formation is complete by the third stage of their cycle. This is known as the resting stage or changing stage where it starts to turn into a butterfly.

Like the butterfly which goes through many twists and turns, and by the very nature of transformation are survivors, so we must be likewise, if we are to find our purpose and live out God's design for our lives. Butterflies are known to have the capacity to adapt and make it through unimaginable circumstances. Butterflies are holometabolous, experiencing a complete metamorphosis, or in other words, a complete change in body form. Moreover, The body of a caterpillar is restructured in its process and formation of becoming a butterfly. Restructuring is key for us too as people of purpose. On the road to purpose our lives become restructured, and/or reordered, as we progress through process into becoming the image and design God has for us

If there is a need to be-come, it follows there must be a pre-transitioning before be-coming, or why would there be the need to become or be like…? The be-coming process is inevitable. It is the beginning of a new chapter on what can sometimes be a long-protracted journey, to becoming the person God desires you to be. For before you were born, he knew you, and knew what you would become. The old you then become the new you, for 'Behold old things have passed away and behold a morphing into the intended person God purposed you to be'. Just like the caterpillar morphs into the butterfly, you now begin to live the life of the person you were created to be.

Let us consider the following parallels:

1.   Therefore, if any man be a new "creature" old thing are passed away and behold (look) all things have become new.

2.   The butterfly be-comes that new creature; in that the newly created thing begins life as a butterfly and functions differently to that of a caterpillar. We too, have a different way of functioning. Now that we have be-come a new creature; we be-come more purpose focused and purpose driven.

3.   Caterpillars do not have wings, but butterflies do. As *butterflies,* God wants us to metaphorically spread our wings and fly and soar and climb the purpose trail. We need to start flying and making ground not crawling around. The word "crawl" suggests and conjures up the image of something that makes slow and sluggish movements. Whereas flying, denotes possessing power and energy, soaring, and attaining. The Bible makes many references to his people 'taking on wings like an eagle'. In the state of a caterpillar, one is not able to do so. The "caterpillar stage" is just the transition stage. We are not meant to remain in that

state. Let us now start to fly.

4. Butterflies lay eggs and pollinate flowers. As purpose focused individuals, we too ought to impregnate others with our vision, permeate the dry areas of our society, make a difference, and have influence as God intended us to. Pollination is a way of extending or empowering or impregnating others with your gift seed.

Butterflies must complete their transition to be able to function differently by flying, pollinating, and replicating themselves to produce more of their kind. Likewise, we cannot impregnate others with the zeal for purpose, and to be-come all that God intended for us to be, if we remain outside the realms of our purpose. We must be transformed into the image of God, as he saw us, and as he has perceived us, if we are to effect and impact others to seek to live out their purpose.

Be-coming one with God and living within the realm of his purpose for our lives, is now our focus. The three following scriptures all speak of God becoming our salvation. In Psalm 118:21 says, "The Lord has become my salvation". The Lord becomes to you what he always intended to be, your salvation. You start to become that person, look that person, behave, and act like that person, and live that person you were created on purpose to be. There is a be-coming because you had a past which did not conform to the image of Christ for your life. Becoming speaks of greater grace to become that person and is a process which moves you from grace to greater grace. Isaiah 12: 2 God has become our Salvation. Essentially, God has become and is becoming, all that you desired for him to become in your life. Psalm 118:14 David needed God to become his Jehovah Nissi, (his banner), his Jehovah Tsideknu (his righteousness), his Jehovah Rapha, (his healer), his Jehovah Jireh (his provider), and his Jehovah Shalom (His Peace). The statement in this verse of scripture shows that David had witnessed the manifestation of God be-coming his salvation to him in the true sense of the word.

Let us be clear in the knowledge that there is a before and after as David clearly demonstrates. The presence of the power of God in one's life enables the process of be-coming to commence. For it is the power of God in his word which brings about the transformation and transition to God's intended place for you. God had become to David that which he had prayed cried and labored for; this is David's testimony. Think of David's life and the areas in which he would have needed God to intervene; for example, fighting selfish thoughts over Bathsheba, in fear of his life and sanity because of Saul's incessant witch hunt against him aimed at alienating him, being side lined by his family and left to mind sheep, being laughed at, and not forgetting, being ridiculed because of his size. In all this, David could finally say, God has become my salvation! Whatever he needed God to be and do for him, David experienced it. The process of salvation is all encompassing, all embracing, and delivers in totality.

It Is Time To Labour

Likewise, we must pull ourselves out when the transition is complete. This is imperative because oftentimes, we can become so submerged by the process that we have no strength left with which to pull or push ourselves through into the new day. But the process is only for a time as it has its season. God keeps us in the confinement, if you like, preparing us while we are so contained, so that when it is time for the 'showcase', he can confidently put us on display. When we are released, the 'new you' makes its appearance, and it will be quite apparent that we have been transformed. What emerges is a stunning beautiful colourful butterfly with the ability to fly, live out its destiny, and soar far above the confinements of its previous life, its struggle, and its old nature. In its' old skin, the caterpillar crawled along and was the underdog. In its' new life, we like the caterpillar are transformed into the butterfly, confident to be on display, with no limitations, and with the ability to soar to new heights, becoming the head and not the tail. Metamorphism is now full and complete.

Now, we have be-come empowered to live out our purpose.

Chapter 2

EMPOWERED

As previously surmised, I believe that we each have a God-given purpose and that we have been equipped with the potential to carry out that purpose. Our life assignment is the reason for our existence in the earth. We are to here influence our generation and impact our society for a reason, a purpose, and a defined season in an era of time, for the Kingdom of God.

Prosperity

Prosperity does not only involve the ability to make money, to get money to work for us, or to become wealthy. I believe, being prosperous embraces the components of tenacity, excellence, leverage, or influence; the ability also to provide a haven of safety and protection and being in good health. When we become prosperous, it is assumed rightly, that we have acquired the foreknowledge and understanding needed, to make the necessary changes to bring about the desired change. It assumes further in the case of living a healthy life, we have the knowledge that we need to eat a healthy balanced diet if we are to set the appropriate foundation for a healthy life in our latter years. The ability to prosper financially assumes we have understood the value of money, the need to have and make wise investments, and that living from paycheck to paycheck, is not the will of God for our lives. Furthermore, prosperity assumes rightly or wrongly, that we as parents have understood the importance, significance, and responsibilities, of providing for the family in terms of the family unit and the protection and safety of our children.

When we arrive at the place of prosperity it is fair to assume we have learned to demonstrate the principles of responsibility and accountability, and we should therefore expect to become the point of reference, or the example, by which others will look up to, hoping for a glimpse of how to make the necessary changes in their own lives. I would say that we owe it to those for whom we have become examples, to live our lives with integrity, justice, fairness, and the desire to empower others. We do not suddenly become entitled because we have become prosperous, but it is imperative to remember our yester-years and retain the knowledge that it is primarily because of our experiences, that we have be-come empowered to live our lives in the prosperous way we do,

Once we have understood the purpose of God, that he has equipped us to prosper, then we are held accountable for the decreed mandate and purpose governing our lives. With the **understanding** of this mandate comes **responsibility,** and with the responsibility there is accountability; **accountability** to others and the people to whom we are destined to impact, and accountability **to God** who has bestowed upon us these gifts.

Too often, it is so easy to apportion blame, or palm responsibility for our misfortunes, on to others. This seems so unfair when we have acquired the necessary knowledge needed to take control and make the right decisions. Yet we still fail to take full responsibility for our actions and seek to find other avenues upon which to vent our frustration. Instead, we should try to identify any shortfalls we may have overlooked or determine whether we failed to strategically plan for the inevitable. As adults we are no longer children tossed back and forth by every whim and idea. We are adults and need to be responsible for our actions and our mistakes. Every action carries a consequence i.e., a result or outcome. It is therefore imperative as much as it is possible, to look at the whole picture of what is involved in anything we do and ensure that we have a back-up plan in place if needed.

Divine Purpose

Divine purpose is God's will for our lives; his purpose being pre-determined before we were even born. We can only come into the knowledge of this purpose by embracing the God who created us and made all things for us to enjoy. He sent his Son Jesus Christ to die in our stead. He became sin for us being sinless himself, that he might reconcile man to himself. This selfless act enables us to be-come empowered to live out our purpose, and to effect change in a world which is crying out for the presence of the Saviour. Some do not yet know Him as the Saviour, but to those who do know him, he is revered as God, Lord, Almighty, and as creator or all things. He desires more than anything else that we prosper and be in good health.

Purpose is the key to the "why's" in life. People are always on a quest to find the meaning to life. The answer TO LIFE is in discovering and then knowing God's design focus and blueprint for our lives.

Destiny

Destiny is God's destined end for us as individuals; the ultimate reason He created us. Destiny runs through the very veins of our life journeys, embodying our life assignment, which is the blueprint of our lives. In turn, this trajectory includes the impact we will have on those whom we encounter, our influence, and our contribution while on earth; to whom where, and when.

Many factors can hinder us from discovering our purpose. Chief among the things that can delay that connection with purpose, is the adverse circumstances which may have shaped and impacted our lives to date. Low self-esteem can be a major detriment to any upward progress in our lives. I have provided points below for those who desire to become empowered and have come to the place of frustration determined now to move on.

Take a walk with me into the counselling room for a moment......................

"You have eroded away at your self-worth because of setbacks in your life disappointments and even failures." It is essential to recreate the image you once had of yourself, as a child, when you embraced aspirations for your future and where life would take you. You then need to re-present this information back to yourself, digest it, and get it into your psyche. These steps are important because, whatever is in your subconscious will manifest itself in your reality.

Can you identify with this scenario? You probably had, or have dreams, where life would take you then the *force* of low self-esteem stopped you in your tracks. You realize that you can no longer pretend that you did not have a problem with low self-esteem. You ask the question, "How am I to deal with this element of negativity? Would I allow its *curse* to determine the course of my life?"

The fact that you are reading this chapter now, and have entered the counselling room with me, signals that you are ready to change and ready to empower someone with the benefit of your experience, having gained victory over this area of your life. It is the emotion of frustration, which has driven you to this posture. This is a good sign, as the emotion of frustration is a powerful tool, because it can act as a catalyst to propel you to take stock of your situation and empower you to re-evaluate your future.

Moving Forward

1. Make a conscious decision to leave behind the past, and find a role model or someone who could possibly mentor you

2. Create and begin to nurture the image that you want to intentionally project. People generally react to what they see and what we portray. Negativity will attract negativity, whereas a positive confident attitude and persona, will cause people to warm and respond more positively towards you.

3. Resist and rebuke negativity; particularly, those who pull you down and constantly slate or judge you; remembering, it is praise and encouragement which builds you up. It is a coward who cannot admit to their own issues with low self-esteem, and who delights in criticizing and ridiculing others to feed their own insecurities.

4. You need to change your mindset and thoughts about yourself. God has not made any mishaps or mistakes. All of us are perfect in his sight. Remember God sees you at the end of your process and not at the beginning and has assigned help to enable you to get there. Better is the end of a thing than the beginning. (Ecclesiastics 7:8)

5. Identify the root of the problem and get help. It is not enough to only deal with the symptoms.

6. Do not allow anyone to define you. Be the one to set your own boundaries remembering that achieving your aims and desires builds confidence.

7. Be prepared to go on a journey of self-discovering to identify with your passion, purpose, and potential; then use those special gifts that are inherent within you.

Note, that many pioneers, role models and successful businesspeople we admire, have used the pain of their past, as steppingstones, to build the future that they desire.

Dream Again............

I would like to admonish those who have entered the counselling room with me, to take a fresh look again at what you want out of life, and begin, even if in brief, to jot down your plans and aspirations, as if absolutely anything was possible. Allow yourself to dream just one more time, to determine whether your experience could be better used, by becoming an advocate for someone whose life mirrors that of your own.

Once you connect with purpose, your whole life, even with the adverse circumstances you have experienced, will take on new meaning. Know this, that your life experience is often indicative of your life- assignment, who you are, where you are; and will inevitably answer, the 'whys' in your life.

We believe as born-again disciples, that Jesus is the counsellor of all counsellors. He knows the intricacies of your make-up, how much you are hurting, and have been hurt. He also has the answers you are looking for.

He uses his sons and daughters i.e., his *ministers,* to help bring restoration to your situation, through the gospel of salvation, the spoken word, and practical assistance.

As mentioned earlier, to connect with our God-given purpose, requires the seeker to become reconnected to God through the gospel of salvation. We do this by accepting him as our Lord and Saviour. He is the one who holds our life span in His hands.

The gospel of salvation is a three-pronged process. It is (a) the process of reconciliation with Jesus Christ, where we become one with Him, and accept Him as the only God in our life; (b) the restoration of one's inner being, this being the chamber of our emotions the *soul-man;* and (c) the empowerment of an individual, so as to enable the person to go out and fulfill their life assignment, purpose and ultimate destiny; your destiny being that thing for which, we (respectively) were created.

Empowerment, therefore, is essential, or else we fail to embrace fully the message of salvation and are in danger of becoming *lame ducks.*

God has a definitive plan for anyone who dares to find out. Moreover, I believe that the gospel of salvation is the only route by which one can reconnect to God and thus ultimately, definitively, and abundantly, live out their purpose. To refer to scripture, the Bible says that "For as many as received him to them gave He power to become the sons of God......." (St. John 1:12). By becoming a son of God, we have access to all that is His; that which He owns and possesses; also, His likeness and creativity. This process involves the principles of be-coming i.e., identifying, emulating, conforming, affirming and ultimately, taking possessing of all that has been destined to us as the Sons, (non-gender specific), of God.

Consider This

How would we have the computer today, or the colour television, or the video recorder or even the car, if someone, somewhere, had not connected to their purpose, or pursued their vision or dream. Such people would have most probably nurtured a passion to be creative, and to give of their best to change their own lives, and the lives of those that work and perhaps live, around them.

It is in times of challenging economic change that God will begin to give us witty ideas of invention, so that we can manifest the glory of God. In these seasons, those who are in covenant relationship with him, will be able to tap into his creativity, and acquire the wisdom to apply the knowledge of that wisdom, to bring about change and sustained prosperity. In the kingdom of God i.e., in the counsel of the forum of believers, it is not who you know that matters, but what you know. Do you have the wisdom and knowledge of God? Do you know the voice God? If you do, then this is all that matters! Even when your money is not safe, or secure in the bank, God will give you the wisdom of where to invest it. You may be directed to invest your money in an invention, or a community venture for example, which will eventually reap, sustained dividends. Our pursuit should be about making a sustained impact, and not about reaping short-lived rewards.

There is so much more to your purpose when you tap into the knowledge of the creator of the universe and of all humanity. Your potential then becomes limitless, with no boundaries, and perhaps, affecting the world over.

Paul, the apostle, in the New Testament Section of the Bible, speaks of his desire to know God in the power of his resurrection. The emphasis being placed on the word POWER. Jesus was resurrected in power! What an awesome life source God's power is! The word **power** in this context, infers a surge of change, a dynamic change or difference; this is the power of the gospel. As Sons of God our lives ought to mirror that of Jesus Christ; and so, as Christ was raised from the dead, we that are raised from our dead works i.e. (the beggarly elements of our life, or non-functioning aspects of our life), should also arise, to walk in *newness* of life.

The Power Of His Resurrection

Consider the following:

> Broken families being restored and receiving the power to start all over again. Abused and battered women overcoming the pain of their pass, to become advocates to others who find themselves in similar circumstances; absent fathers finding the love and self-respect to forge

new links with their children.

These and many more, are prime examples of people becoming empowered by their experience. Likewise, the scenario of the resurrection of Christ from the dead is to be compared to that of a *new birth; a second chance if you like, or another crack at the whip,* but with a new focus and mindset. As we arise out of a situation, we become empowered having left the past behind, and now face life with a new vigour, determination, and power. This does not necessarily mean that we may never face another challenge, but we become better equipped next time around, because of the experience of having overcome.

There is power to be accessed through the impartation of our experience to others, because as they too become over-comers, we are strengthened in our resolve, knowing that our experience has not been in vain. We are also confident in the knowledge that we were able to turn that same experience to our advantage.

Many a million $ has been acquired by others because of the pain of failing or going bankrupt (not that I am advocating that we purposefully choose to). However, those who have been challenged in this way have never allowed this setback to be the last word in their lives. They have simply got up, dusted themselves off, and started all over again!

The disciples of Jesus having been with Jesus, and become empowered by their experience, were placed in a position which harnesses and imparts, that same power, to those who became the recipients of their ministering. This is so clearly illustrated in the New Testament book of Mark 16:15 where Jesus after been raised from the dead said unto his disciples "Go ye into all the world and preach the gospel to every creature......." Also, in the New Testament book of John 15:27, wherein the disciples were able to testify of the power of the gospel, because they had been with Jesus from the beginning.

Because we have amassed a wealth of experience through our past failings, we are much more effectively placed to help and minister to others. Paul, one of the contributors to several the New Testament books, reiterates this point when he said, "All things work together for your good." (Romans 8:28). Our experience may not be good of itself, but the nature of the experience can work together for our good, by making us more resilient, tenacious, and focused.

It Is Time For The Manifestation Of The Power God

Consider this statement

"The person who the *world* has rejected has become the successor and the major player." – an excerpt taken from the Book of Mathew.

i.e., the stone which the builders had rejected has become the chief corner stone
(Matthew 21:42; Mark 12:10; Luke 20:17)

If there was ever a poignant time in Christendom, it is now, where we as the ministers of Christ, the church, need to begin to redefine our relationship with God. The whole Kingdom message is to empower others. For Christ came that we might have life, and life more abundantly. Are we being empowered by the gospel messages, which are so readily preached and skillfully propagated, and which echo weekly from our local church communities? Are lives being changed to enable people to live the life that Jesus came to give; or are our congregations returning home, to lives that remain unchanged, though their commitment to the 'faith' as they know it, remains undiminished? Those who propagate the gospel of Salvation, have an **obligation** to empower people with the Kingdom message. Ponder this point, are we fulfilling our mandate, or will our labouring have been in vain?

It is time to trade in the dependency attitude for one that creates equal opportunities, gives knowledge, and offers constructive support, and not handouts. People need the knowledge of how to get out of a situation and ought not to be controlled by certain mindsets and principalities. Failure to do so will render a continuing need for such persons to keep coming back to others, as their source of help and support, instead of identifying what resources they have at their disposal to help themselves. The source of our own wealth is often in our own hands. However, we often need the help and support to identify this. Therefore, a message preached without a method is a mess. People need to know how to......, where to......, who to......., and to be given counsel and direction. Those without knowledge are often blind to the way out of their situation. Knowledge gives power, and power gives influence, and the ability to do for oneself, something which may have been denied because of a previous lack of foresight and knowledge. People need to be equipped with the tools to get the job done.

How does one teach a child, or expect a child to learn, if that child is not at least shown how to do the task, that is being asked of him or her? Similarly, if you give a person a fish you feed that person for that moment in time only. But if you show the person how to fish, or fend for themselves, then they have an opportunity to acquire the skills to be able to fend for themselves for all time.

Motivational speakers often give examples of success stories and illustrate the basic principles of goal setting and task prioritization etc. i.e., how to move from one level to another. Similarly, we as preachers may be perceived as "motivational speakers". Within this context, there is a lot to be said about educating the believer or the church, with the tools to lay the foundation or to create an environment, which is conducive to sustained growth. The taught word is meant to enlighten as to how to......, what do we do in each situation? How do we get from where we are to where we need or desire to be?

It is all right to shout. It is all right to dance and sing joyously, but what happens when the dance and the singing comes to an end, and we go home to our respective homes, and we retire to bed. The light is turned off, and we lie there with our own thoughts racing through our minds. We have all been there. We went to church today, but what did we learn? Church or the coming together of a body of people, is a time for learning, for fueling up for the week ahead, and a time for gathering pointers and help, to enable us to set our goals and move towards our purpose.

We that have become sons of God, having become empowered by the gospel of salvation, need to demonstrate this life saving gift of salvation, by being an example of the word in deed and in action. Our life must be our testimony, our witness, and an example of the empowering grace of Jesus Christ. God desires to see the manifestation of his work in our daily lives.

The baton is in our hands; we have been given the

opportunity to set the precedent, lay the foundation, and leave a legacy for those who should follow us.

What Will They Say About YOU After You Have Gone?

We all individually, and collectively, have a contribution to make to our world, which no one else can make, but YOU!

Chapter 3

IT IS NOT MONEY YOU NEED IT IS FAVOUR

The gospel of salvation is a gospel of evidence. People are only interested in how much you have be-come enabled by the grace of God, and not necessarily how much you know. Similarly, people are affected by what they see. One's faith is tangible, and it is the tangible manifestation of God's effect upon our lives, which validates our faith. It is time for the people of God to be put on display. God intends to boast himself through us, as we manifest his power and his glory. Now that a new day has dawned, we have the keys to unlock the doors to change.

Favour will take you, where money cannot buy you influence or an audience with the Queen of England, or indeed, the President of the United States of America for example. Money cushions us in the eventuality, but if it is favour you need, then this is a job for God. God is the one that provides the link, like no other can. Favour will promote you, and give you leverage and influence in high places, where money cannot even go the distance.

It is not money you need it is favour!

Too many times we say, "if only I had the money, then I would do this or that;" Money is only the vehicle by which we can move operate or trade. However, it does not necessarily facilitate the trade itself, without having the right connection or opportunity.

It is in knowing who to call, whom to contact, knowing which person is best placed to exert proper influence to get the job done. This chain of events does not even involve an exchange of currency. It is simply called favour. We need favour that others will take note of our skills and expertise within a given area. We need favour so that when they need a job doing, we are the one who receives the call for help, to the extent, that we become the one component, without which, the job cannot be done.

What Is Favour?

Favour is to be granted or to be placed in a position, to take advantage of an opportunity, which would not otherwise have been afforded to us, either because of the lack of the requisite qualifications, experience, or service. Favour is about being able to obtain something just for the mere fact that we were in the right place at the right time; an opportunity which was either unmerited or for which, we may remain unqualified, but nevertheless yet given the opportunity, has come our way. Favour makes itself known, or apparent, when we understand our season and then, being enabled or postured to network with others.

Favour will even work for you where money has no value.

With favour comes honour and promotion. There are essentially five steps to honour and promotion. These are:

1. The presence of Godly influence
2. The ability to exercise financial and business integrity
3. Divine favour, providential circumstance; and Strategic positioning
4. Honoring God
5. Divine revelations.

The Presence Of Godly Influence

Having Godly influence gives one the leverage of veto when circumstances may indicate otherwise. Godly influence allows one to have influence, when and where it is needed most. For example, in a life challenging situation, in a hopeless situation, and in a life-or-death situation, and especially in a situation, where only God can intervene to bring about the desired result.

Financial And Business Integrity And Fidelity

Financial and business integrity and fidelity is the ability to exercise the upmost integrity, to the point of not succumbing to unscrupulous business practices. This applies to managing the business of others for example, those for whom we work, and proving, that we can be both trustworthy and honest.

Financial and business integrity, and fidelity, also involves the care and shepherding of the business affairs of others as if it were our own. Being faithful in someone's *"vineyard,"* will reap untold favour and prosperity, when we are placed in the position of having our own *"vineyard"*

One may find oneself in a position of temptation, yet not tempted to breach certain principles; preferring instead, to live by an ethical code of conduct. Consider for example, the biblical character of Joseph who encapsulates what it means to operate with financial integrity. Joseph found himself in plush surroundings and indeed he was a stranger to such surroundings, and one who others would say, was out of his depth. Yet as a stranger, and one that did not belong in a palace, he was promoted to second in command in Pharaoh's house. Notably, it is well documented that Joseph acted with the upmost integrity and propriety.

One's humility is also tested, when what would seem like a golden opportunity, presents itself; an opportunity which may not quite follow the business rules of ethical conduct. I refer to the incident with Potiphar's wife, who incredulously believed, that Joseph would succumb to her charms. Maybe others would have done so; perhaps, to obtain favours, or opportunities, which may not naturally have come their way. However, we note that Joseph acted with the utmost integrity.

Divine Favour Strategic Positioning And Providential Circumstance

Divine Favour

Defined as obtaining something for which you are not qualified for or do not possess the requisite criteria for. Divine favour embraces the concepts of providential circumstance and strategic positioning.

Strategic Positioning

God hides us in the *mess* until the appointed time. He has positioned us on purpose, ready to be revealed at his appointed time. It is often the cause of a providential circumstance, which can catapult us from where we are in the 'doldrums', to our place of destiny. The dictionary describes the word **providential** as having foresight, being thrifty, being fortunate or lucky. Being in the position of providential circumstance merits the need for knowledge foresight and wisdom and can catapult us into a position of influence; especially so when favour has placed us into a position to be noticed. We would not be in this position had it not been for the favour of God. Consider the examples of Joseph,

Daniel, and Moses.

Reflecting on the journey of Joseph (Genesis 39:20), we can see where he would have still been languishing in a prison cell, if it were not for providential circumstance - in that Pharaoh needed someone who could interpret dreams. As we read in the book of Genesis, it was Joseph's God given ability to interpret dreams which got the attention of Pharaoh, which resulted in him being released from prison, and eventually catapulting him into his destiny, as ruler in Pharaoh's house. In Pharaoh's house he was positioned to deliver Egypt from famine and to preserve the posterity of Israel in the earth by saving his family – "for in thy seed shall all the nations of the earth be blessed". Genesis 26:4.

A time will come when there will be a providential circumstance, like there was with Joseph, which will propel you into your destiny. You will be the person at the right place at the right time to fulfill that need. That person will see in you, what God desires them to see, his blueprint for your life. In the book of Genesis Chapter 39:2 when Pharaoh saw that God made all that Joseph did to prosper in his hand, he made him ruler (or commander in chief), in his household. The chapter says he was a prosperous man, and he was in the house of his master. This was unusual because Joseph was a Jew and Pharaoh an Egyptian as referred to above. Nevertheless, Joseph's master Pharaoh, saw that the Lord was with him and that the Lord made all that he did to prosper in his hand. Accordingly, Joseph found grace in Pharaoh's sight, and he made him overseer over his house and all that he had he put into his hand. We note from the scripture that the Lord blessed the Egyptians house for Joseph's sake, and the blessing of the Lord was upon all that Pharaoh possessed.

People will do things for you, when under 'normal' circumstances, they would not have had any contact with you. Divine favour and providential circumstance will do this for you. When others see the influence and impact that we have on their business, organization, the ministry etc., the resulting affect will be the exercise of favour which will open doors for us. Moreover, the *gift* that God has placed in us, will open doors of opportunities for us.

Many of us may have become devalued as a direct

result of misfortune and adverse circumstances. Devalued to the point where we have unintentionally misrepresented, or under-represented, the gift of God within us, for what seems like, forever. It is now though, time to get ready for the change of pace, so that when the overflow comes, we have a new mind-set and can start receiving what God has to offer. We need to change our mind-set, from lack to abundance, otherwise, we will continue to belittle ourselves, and not be postured to receive or accept, what God desires to give us.

On examining the story of Daniel, we see where his gift brought him before Kings, as he was gifted with all manner of wisdom and understanding. The King Nebuchadnezzar needed a man that could interpret his dreams. Daniel was the only one who could do so. The King had effectively removed all the wise men of the day, and had put out a warrant for their death, because none of the so-called wise men of the day, could interpret the dream which had by now begun to trouble Nebuchadnezzar. We see Daniel's gift opened opportunities for him, and subsequently he was strategically positioned at the right place, and at the right time for promotion.

We look at Moses, who was running from away from his past after killing the Egyptian. Moses was called by God, to go back to Egypt, and positioned by God, to bring the children of Israel out of Egypt. Moses was equipped with favour (power) to deliver God's chosen people, and to show forth the glory of God within the Egyptian Empire.

Honoring God

When God has moved us out of, and into, the *land* of prosperity, we need to remember to honour God for his faithfulness to us. Even those who have not reconciled with God or become heirs of the Kingdom of God, recognize the need to pay homage to his favour, and care over their lives. Many unbelievers feel the need to repay the kindness of grace, by either giving to charity or donating a percentage of their earnings, to the Church.

Divine Revelations

Having Infinite foresight, insight, knowledge, and wisdom is to be totally one with God. In this position, we will be empowered to do great exploits for the Kingdom of God. It is possible to get to this posture in life. In times of economic crises, a word of direction that is loaded with revelation and insight as to the way forward, is what is needed. Provision for an economy in crises, is discernible through taking hold of the vision as received, through time spent with God. The custodians of this plan then must be communicated in a way which can facilitate change, to compass the way forward.

Chapter 4

THE DAWNING OF A NEW DAY

(A Letter To The Church – The Ministers Of The Gospel of Jesus Christ)

It is good to remember Egypt, but Egypt it is not a place we should desire or want to go back to or remain in. We can visit it now and then, to draw or reflect upon our experiences, but it should not be our intention to remain there. If we challenge the system that has kept us in bondage, we will change it.

Egypt is metaphorically used as an example to illustrate our days of struggle, often remembered, or defined as a bitter-sweet experience; more bitter, than sweet though. We are now in a new day, where divine counsel will be sought from many, including political parties to financial institutions, as people grapple with diverse and challenging times. If ever there was a time for the church to shine their light, it is now. The church can do so by offering wise and Godly counsel, just like in the days of Daniel and Joseph.

A process of redressing the balance is about to happen. The church will no longer be the underdog but the top dog. The vision should now be clear that many opportunities have presented themselves to the church, and the Church should be equipped to minister to those in need.

The Church needs to demonstrate an atmosphere of growth and prosperity. by being an example in the way we live, conduct itself, and the standards that we adhere to. It is to the Church that the pillars of society i.e., the government, the major corporate and legislative institutions, schools, and other governing bodies, should refer to, when seeking wise council - just as in the days of Daniel, Joseph and even more recently, in the last century, John Wesley.

There is a new meaning to "train up a child in the Way that he should grow, and when he is old, he shall not depart from it". If we re-phrase this verse, it could read like this:

'Teach a man how to fish and he will develop the skills to fish for a lifetime'.

Put yet another way; empower and equip others to lead, to be accountable, to take on responsibility, and to move away from the position of being ego-centric i.e., that selfish attitude which is gnawing away at many of our churches today.

We need not to be sitting up in lack, when abundance is ours to be gained through the infinite wisdom of God; for truly the scripture says that those of the world are wiser than those in relationship of God. In layman terms, the Church have God as their father, and therefore being in "the know", should be wiser! (St. Luke 16:8).

Egypt Or The Land Of Promise?

The church should not be about receiving handouts, but it should be about giving out. We therefore need to *put to bed,* that slave mentality in order that we can see the harvest of souls and provide the answers to the desperate cry of a world in need. There are many seeking after the purpose of life and a quest to find the answers to *"why am I here?"* Feeding time at the Zoo is over; the spectators pen is full and cannot seat anymore. Those who are on the outside of the feeding pen need to get out of their comfort zones and leave Egypt to those who have no intention of making their mark in this world, contributing to society, or to the

Kingdom of God. How does the Church prove the power of God should they be content to sit in a comfort zone, when God is calling the Church to travail through *deeper waters*? It is time for the church to slay the spirit and attitude of mediocrity and start applying the wisdom of God, by tapping into the infinite power of God.

There are those, who having just started out on this journey, aspire to know God explore their faith, and reach out for the best that God has to offer. Whilst there may be others who are seasoned in the faith, who unfortunately have got caught up in an agenda of nothing-ness, debating about meaningless ideologies, ever learning but never graduating, and are content to sit down and do nothing! As the corporate body of Christ, we should endeavour to come together and unite and avoid the angst of separation and division. After all, there is more which unites us as a body of believers despite our theological differences, than those things which threaten to divide us! A Kingdom divided against self-renders itself to becoming weak, *sitting down to everything, and not standing up for anything*! We need to learn to unite on the things we agree about and agree to differ peaceably and amicably about the things that we disagree about. We need to get a paradigm shift and start to look at things differently. Where is our domain? Where is our Kingdom? What changes are we actively seeking to implement? Every other facet in society seems to have something they care passionate enough about, to campaign for, but the Church seems not to! The Church does not appear to actively campaign for anything! If we challenge the things, we passionately care about, we will create the platform for change.

In Egypt God fed watered and clothed us, but we the believers are no longer in Egypt, but as empowered people, our mission now is to empower others. In this position of empowerment, we are going to need to remember what we learnt in our process whilst we were in *Egypt* i.e., tenacity, self-discipline, determination, stoicism, to keep the momentum pace, and advancement, as we progress in our purpose and in our place of promise, *the wealthy place*. This *place* of promise is a place of authority, dominion, and accountability.

As empowered believers, it is all about favour and doors of opportunities being opened to us and moreover, recognizing these opportunities in the knowledge, that they are to be exploited to the full. (i.e., taken to their full advantage). However, if we cannot see such opportunities, how do we even begin to go after them? If we can only but see the invisible, with our spiritual eyes, we can do the impossible. As the body of believers, we need to pray that our eyes become anointed that we can see the purpose and will of God. Competition and opposition will come our way, but we would have learnt to deal with such foes while we were in our process in Egypt, so that these challenges should come as no surprise to us!

Our Attitude Determines Our Altitude

Joshua in berating the mentality of the second generation of Israel said, "Why do you take so long to possess the land- seeing it stands before you?" Joshua 18:3 The sojourners still had their minds in Egypt, with the "give me, give me" attitude, instead of "I'm going after it" attitude. I suppose it takes more to stand up and fight for what is ours, our inheritance through our covenant with God, than to sit down, and succumb to our circumstances. But if we be kings and priests and joint-heirs with Christ, then we must be in possession of a Kingdom, and if not, then we are falling short of the "high-calling of God" Philippians 3:14. God did not call us to be beggars. Our relationship with God needs to change from one of servitude, or servant hood, to one of sonship; because Jesus said "I call you not servants but sons, as the servant knows not what his Lord does" St. John 15:15. Furthermore, a servant is at the mercy of his slave master, but a Son is conscious of, and embraces, the promise of his inheritance, and receives favour from his Father.

Why have we not progressed or advanced forward enough? Is it because the Church have not stood for anything? It is time to wake up faith, for the time has come for the Church to become a consultant to nations.

The Equation Of Challenge

If we as the Body of Christ challenge the generational curses that bind some of our believers, and challenge the *spirit* of mediocrity, which can, and has so often, been allowed to permeate mould and shape our churches, we will have the power and leverage to change our families, impact a lineage, re-charge our communities and even a whole nation.

The defining moment is when we realize who God is to

us and subsequently who God is in us; for He created us in his image and in his likeness with the power and ability to do as He did. For he said in the New Testament Book of St. John Chapter 14:12; "Greater works than these shall you do". I.e., greater works than we have seen him do as he has shown and demonstrated in the scriptures.

Chapter 5

LIVING OUTSIDE THE BUBBLE

Imagine; capture the image...... *People like rats* running to and fro for underground trains which leave every three to four minutes; hopping on to buses which meander in and out of depots at set times - are leaving their footprints and mark everywhere.

A myriad of figures dressed in suits walk around importantly as their voices can be heard booming over the tannoy at the stock exchange and money market centres. Whoever coined the phrase "the rat race" quite aptly, depicted humans converging together in a bid to get somewhere in a hurry; that somewhere never really bringing satisfaction but invariably leaving, uncertainty, disillusionment despair, and chaos, in its wake!

Is this the beginning of the end of the get rich quick schemes, the property boom, and of making a fast buck on the stock market? Is this the end of the drudgery of getting up to go to work, at the sound of the chimes, as our respective alarm clocks go off, on yet another dark winter's day? It is not that we have an unhealthy work ethic - but more of a case of the value or significance we place on what we do, for the best part of our lives, 9 -5pm with an hour for lunch. Is this it? Is life all about trying to survive, keeping up with the Jones's, having the latest gadgets, and whilst at the same time being satisfied for just a mere moment, but never having any lasting satisfaction or contentment? Is it about always striving, and yet not knowing what we are striving for, and at the same time questioning if there is more to life than this! This is life within the bubble, a life of routine, and just so. But then.......................

Imagine the scenario; Dark days, foggy times, and headlines depicting more economic gloom, radiates from the broad sheets of today's papers. Newspapers illuminated by the dim light on the train as commuters make their daily ride home from work. Such news is becoming common place as the month's progress. What does this mean for the man in the street, struggling to survive and feed his family, and maintain a roof over his head? Consider the corporate businessman - a millionaire in fact, who is on the verge of taking a decision he has never had to make in his life. The storm of adversity avalanches. No-one is exempt; from the corporate investment banker to the postman, as a trail of devastation lies in its wake. Does this herald the end of the rat race as we all know it? Is this the time for one to spend quality time with families, and a time to take life at a slower place, thereby adding real time and value to the concept we call, living?

I believe it is time to re-think our strategies. Who wants to be part of the rat race anyway? It is time to dig our heels in. We are in this for the long haul. We will survive if we know the value of trusting the One who has created all things, knows all things, and who has the wisdom to unlock the strategies needed to renew, and restore those things, which the storm has caused to become broken.

Presently there may be many of us living inside the bubble assured of our protection and safety, putting our trust in horses, chariots; whatever goes! Like clockwork, we go to work, do the weekly shop, busy ourselves with the daily chores, and all without a hint of excitement or challenge. There is something awry with this modicum attention to the way we live our lives, and this is the failure to ensure that we are covered in the event of a *rainy day*. Times are changing and it is not business as usual. Seat belts have had to be tightened, purse strings restrained, new concepts have been coined, like the need to conserve our *carbon footprints*. This change can impact our lives, like a wakeup call does, creating an awareness and mindfulness to create, reinstate, and re-emphasis in all of us, the need to value what we have, use our resources wisely, and become better stewards of those things which we are privileged to possess. This is a season of challenge, and without being asked, many of us have been presented with the opportunities to make a lasting change, take a change of direction, and find the meaning and purpose to our lives; the God given purpose which brings true contentment and satisfaction. This change of life epitomizes living outside the bubble.

Many believers who have become born again to a living faith, are not necessarily perturbed by the advent of the recent timeline of events, simply because they are not living in a false economy. Instead, we are trusting in the economy of heaven which does not rely on superficial financial spurts funded by borrowed money, and the misconception that fulfillment in life consists in the abundance of the things we possess. There are no economies of scale in the Kingdom of God. The currency now used for trading in these changing times, are the principles of creativity, favour, mercy, and unconditional love. Remember money is only the currency vehicle in which we operate. However, money cannot operate independently of our time, God-given creativity, or favour.

Without the plan or creative idea, money does not even begin to come into the equation. I am not advocating that as believers we do not need to plan, but the fear factor of the "what might be", or the unpredictable of "what if", has been taken away, and replaced by peace. As believers we believe that God, whose wisdom is infinite, and supersedes that of the most eminent of scholars, has the answers needed to remedy and challenge the problems we may face. In the Kingdom of God there is no recession; the economy remains unshaken. Do not misunderstand me; this does not mean that money will literally fall from heaven, but God can impart to us by way of new strategies and his wisdom, the "how to", needed to tackle the problems that pervade our world, communities. and society generally. An exchange needs to take place, where we replace the wisdom of man, with the wisdom of God. Furthermore, when we can admit that we no longer have the answers to bring about sustained change, then God will be so happy to step in, and impart his wisdom and the understanding of how to apply the knowledge of this wisdom. He is waiting on us to make that call.

The bubble that many of us have been living in has provided a false economy, and a false sense of security, allowing for the delusion of flatteries and briberies to entertain us. Many are falling prey to underhand practices, and unbridled greed, in the belief that we have got by before unnoticed, so it does not matter. Under this false rain cloud, it is so easy to throw on complacency and the cloak of being protected by conceitedness and self-deception, whereby we ultimately repulse the common principle of decency and integrity. For those, for whom the bubble has burst, take time to ponder this sobering thought. Your business now is one of learning how to survive and live outside the bubble.

Outside the bubble we are offered no protection to cushion our fall should we fall or fail, and some of us may need to learn how to fight again for our survival, dig our heels in, and learning perhaps again, the basic tools of survival. We may be forced out of our comfort zone, just like a newborn fledging learning how to fly for the very first time. This can be no mean feat, as I have said earlier in the book, that many of those who have been successful, have made many mistakes, and failed but have used their past experiences to build the future they have today. But it is by no means the end - what else is in your hand? What is the sum value of your worth?

Today, those who know the grace and favour of God will be the ones who, whilst during the storm, will increase in strength and faith, retain their integrity and good character and above all, see the mighty hand of God come through for them. For them, God is not a stranger they met on the off chance, on a dark night when they were lost on the M1, or someone who they called upon on when hit by a terminal illness, or someone for whom they only acknowledged the existence of, at Christmas time. For them, God has and continues to be, a lifelong friend, someone with whom they have a steady sustained relationship with, and who has been there for them all the way and is involved in every aspect of their lives. It is highly unlikely that many of us would, without the basis of a sustained friendship, (based on trust and longevity), offer a hand up, or a hand of support in the time of crises to others, including casual acquaintances or complete strangers even. God will though. He is, and always will be there, for whosever will.

There is a well-known proverbial, which states that when the going gets tough, the tough get going. I want to add my own slant to this, and say that when times get tough, those who know their God will look to God, and make demands from God. God in turn will show forth his glory in a way that will have all the hallmarks of His intervention.

Many people have trusted in their *horses* (when placing their bets) and in their gods. Some trusted in *safe investments,* while others have turned to soothsayers, and the use of crystal balls, and clairvoyants, in the thirst for knowledge. But it is the survival of the fittest, that will outrun them all! The fittest I deem to be those who are in relationship with God, and God, as the omnipotent being, sees all things, and has already out run all those, who dare to compete with him. The beauty with God is the privilege of coming into covenant relationship with him, an invitation which is open to all. However, the sadness is that there are some of us who have yet to embrace his covenant, and to know the depths of his mercy and love. One thing we must remember though, is that God means us no harm. His desire is to prosper us, and he really does know what is best for us, and desires only to be in covenant relationship with us. God's love for us is like that of a mother's love towards their child; the mother who because of the experience of their own past, tries to steer their child away from repeating the mistakes that they have made. Most parents desire the best for their child because they know only too well, the pain of their own past mistakes, and subsequently become very protective, of their own children.

There was a time when the church and the governments worked in unison; the church being placed in a position to offer advice and counsel. Kings such as King James I of the fifteenth century a defender of the Faith, believed in the principles of the Bible and passed legislation that the Bible should be translated and made available to ordinary people. He also endorsed the use of the Bible as the yardstick for Godly counsel and government. The Bible became the foundation for his government. We see too, that King

David and Samuel the Prophet being in covenant relationship with God, were effectively placed to give advice on all matters concerning the Kingdoms in which they lived. It is time for the return for the likes of people like Smith Wigglesworth, and John Wesley who because of the lives they led, caused a whole generation of people to love God.

It is at this current time of adverse change and when we are faced with an ill wind which appears to be blowing irrespectively in all directions, that as believers, we realize the true value of our faith.

Outside the bubble life is more exciting, and offers new opportunities which we would miss, if we remained cocooned within the bubble. The bubble being the humdrum of life as we have known it. How many of us are up for the challenge? The challenge of investing in new opportunities, where the value of our wealth is not necessarily measured in monetary terms. Wealth is much more than money. I would say being in good health is equal to one being wealthy; and yet it is impossible to put a value or price on good health.

When we walk in the knowledge and wisdom of God,

we are truly wealthy, because what is intrinsically being birthed through the application of these principles, is something which is of more value than rubies or diamonds or gold, simply because our lives will have been changed for the better. There is a need to return to a society where the sanctity of life is restored, and people readily acknowledge the grace mercy, and favour, of a loving God. One who is forgiving and forgives, and one who commands the storms to be still. One whose word is obeyed, and moreover, one who restores order and peace to all.

Chapter 6

IN WHOM DO YOU TRUST?

We trust the mechanic to carry out the repairs to our cars with due care and attention and without fiddling us.

We trust our doctors implicitly to accurately diagnose us when we are ill and prescribe the right medication to treat us. We trust the accounts departments at our respective places of employment to correctly calculate our rate of pay, and to ensure our monthly salaries are paid in time into our bank accounts. We trust our spouses to be loyal, and faithful, and to commit their undying love to us until death separates you. We trust that the children, if we have any, will grow up to be responsible adults, and lead rewarding purposeful and productive lives. We trust that when we retire to bed at night that we will instinctively wake up the following morning, to start the routine all over again, and join the rat race to work. We trust that our jobs are secure, and that redundancies could happen to others but consider it to be inconceivable that the same fate could befall us.

We trust that our financial investments are safe, and that under the law of financial return we will make a healthy return on our investment.

However, there may come a time when everything we can, and do trust in, will no longer sustain us, and we may find ourselves going down with that very thing, we have placed our trust in. Why? because that thing may have lost its security, its value, its sustainability, and can no longer be relied upon.

We place the value of our trust in so many things and in different ways, but who or what cushions us in the event of failure? Upon what premise is our basis of trust founded? Is it the trust and faith in humanity, and the utilitarian principle of the common good of man? Remember, people are subject to change!

It is plausible for someone to operate in the most ordinary way, and ten years down the line, become depressed or suffer a change of character and end up committing some heinous crime. What becomes of our trust then, or the thing we were trusting in? Some of the things we are trusting for, are not dependent on the abilities of others, like our health for example, waking up in the morning, or the money markets. All these things are subject to a myriad of variables. What happens when there appears to be a glitch in the money market and the economy goes into free fall, and the prices of the shares start plummeting? Nothing is ever secure or constant. We are only assured of one thing in life (and morbid though it sounds), and that is death. We all, at some point, will die one day.

It could be argued that for some of us, the foundation of our trust is tangible, perhaps because we know the person dealing with the repairs to our car for example, to be an honest hardworking guy, who has never let you down before.

It should be possible to define or acknowledge that thing in which we are placing our trust. As for the believers, and in this context, I am referring to those who are born again into salvation, and have accepted the love of God, their trust is placed in almighty God; a supernatural spirit, which cannot be seen with the naked eye, but we believe, was in the embodiment of man, and born to a virgin named Mary. This same person, became our Saviour, lived on the earth, over two thousand years ago, and came down to earth to offer salvation redemption and to make an everlasting covenant with humanity.

We can establish therefore, that most of us regarding the very many aspects of life, have placed our trust in a person, the basis of this trust, being the character of the person, and our past experiences with this person. By nature, we rely on what we can see with the natural eye. Therefore, as people of vision, we need to know that we can quantify with the natural eye, that thing we are hoping or trusting in. But what happens in the event of the inexplicable, the unexpected, or the unpredictable?

Is it that hard to trust in that which we cannot see; a God who is able to hold the universe together, who holds the sun in the sky, causes the day and night to come into order, and has given us all things to enjoy, being the creator and originator of all things? If we acknowledge that the Bible is the undeniable word of God, given to us as a tool for salvation, and which contains the principles of how to live a purposeful life, then surely, we can believe in the existence of God as the all-seeing, and all-knowing, ever-present God. The

Bible has stood the test of time. It is the one book throughout the whole of the universe, that has been reprinted over, and over, again. Thousands have attested to its authenticity, validity, and practical relevance to everyday life. There is no other book in the entire universe that is more widely read, than the Bible.

There will be many who have picked up the Bible on the off chance, and have found solace, inspiration, and hope, within its pages. There are many who have faced the challenge of a terminal illness, or an adverse situation for example, who have called out "if there is a God up there - then help", and God has been forthcoming with help.

Conversely, there may be many who may be reading this book, who have not yet openly declared themselves believers, and perhaps do not regularly read the Bible or attend church, but whether consciously or subconsciously, embrace many of the principles contained in the Bible.

Many adhere to the principles of for example, showing compassion to our fellow man, the principle of treating others like we would like to be treated, activating the principles of honesty and integrity – all of which are biblical principles. Why don't we go that one step further and start placing our trust in God? At least that way, we can say that we have taken the step to prove, or disprove, the existence of God, and whether we can affirm, God really is there for us.

If God decrees something, know that he is well able to accomplish and complete his plan, without our aid, if he so desires. Why then is it that we feel unable to trust in God, simply, because we cannot tangibly see him at work. Know then that he works in the unknown, and in secret, 'behind the scenes', if you like, and then displays his work in public, that all can see.

Who saw him at work when he formed the earth? Who witnessed him when he declared the night from the day? Who witnessed him when he created the moon stars and the sun? If you are waiting on him to fulfill a promise, he made to you, rest assured that he knows how to knit the plan together, who to contact and when, and yes, he will be on time! The question you need to ask yourself is do you trust God to work it out for you?

It is a faith thing; but exercising faith is the belief that what we are doing, will result in the change needed to progress forward. Note the emphasis is on the <u>doing.</u> Faith cannot work alone. The principle of faith without action is unfruitful; just like wishing that you could fly off to the Netherlands, but not bothering to apply for a passport to do so and thereafter going on to purchase a ticket so you can make your journey. The scriptures declare "faith without works is dead-faith". The kind of attitude where one says I am waiting on God, but at the same time doing nothing, is what I would call "wishful thinking", which gets one, nowhere fast. It is a misguided person who says well I have believed God but have not actively done anything in support of their belief. God works with what we have. What the misguided person is saying, is they may have perhaps prayed, and then sat down waiting for something to fall from the sky, or a voice to boom out from the shadows. To those people I ask the question, what were you doing with your time while you were seeking God for direction?

Believers are intelligent people, educated, and well informed; be not persuaded by the misconception, that Christ-centered people, Christian or Believers, call them what you may, are otherwise but.........! Many of us as Christ-centered people hold highly powered responsible positions in the city of commerce, finance, and politics. We also are Premiers of Countries, Governments, are pioneering entrepreneurs, and are not, people who have a lazy attitude towards life or, a 'can't be bothered attitude'. Laziness is not a principle of Christian living. In fact, the Bible frowns upon such behavior.

One's faith is built up over time. Faith is not a one-minute wonder. Our faith may also be tested in adverse times; but if the things we are pursuing are things worth fighting for, we simply fight on. As an entrepreneur fighting to maintain their business, or win over a contract, - we will pull out all the stops and not fall at the first hurdle or succumb to challenges because things have become tumultuous. We will look at other options, or avenues, to reach our target or to get the thing done. It is a faith fight, with the premise of that fight being entrenched in the principles of Godly faith, and not merely on verbalizing fighting talk. Such faith fuelled people act; action which is fuelled by the wisdom of God, and which must bring results. Endurance coupled with the knowledge of how to wield the wisdom, and knowledge of God (remembering that

God sees ahead of time and into the future), is the key that is needed now to tackle the challenges we face.

The Bible exhorts us to ask God for the nations, so that he can bestow his wisdom in directing, and preventing, total calamity and financial meltdown, or destruction. Furthermore, we are exhorted to ask God the way forward in times of crises. However, the old proverbial 'it takes a friend to know a friend', is a complicit component in being able to tap into the knowledge, and wisdom of God. If we do not know how God speaks to his subjects, and this he does through many ways for example through his word, through signs, and through his disciples i.e., his followers, then we cannot even begin to understand his direction and wisdom for these times of challenge. A solid relationship is built over time. If you have not already done so, why not start building your relationship with God; then you too can benefit in knowing a God who can provide counsel and direct you.

This current climate could be awesome for the corporate church, to witness the power of God move in a way that is unprecedented in our time. We cannot afford to lose heart, or hope, and settle for nothing, when we profess to believe in a God, who can do exceedingly, abundantly, above all, that we ask or can think. A God who we know can do the possible, where even the impossible, is unthinkable, or unimaginable. We cannot afford to take our eye off the things of God. To do so would mean, adopting belief systems which are not helpful in building our faith. If we are going to keep on believing in the vision, or promise God has placed in our hearts, then we need to guard our hearts against negativity. We cannot afford to draw back, and become demoralized, but remain calm and focused. Do not panic!

We need to find our peace and quiet, or we may end up making or taking decisions which, we would not otherwise have.

There is nothing about the word of God which will cause us to lose heart or hope. Embracing the belief systems of the world, will. Negative statements of doom and gloom, with no prospect of recovery or counsel, are counterproductive to the growth of our faith. The reality of a situation or predicament is what it is, i.e., "the reality of it". Remember however, God by his power, can confound even the direst of circumstances, with results that remain only unimaginable, to the unbeliever! Therefore, we must not allow the size of the opposing factors, or rumours of doom and gloom, to challenge our position, or belief systems, or cause us to lose heart!

To those still sitting on the fence, undecided about the need to allow the love of God to overshadow your life...., I hear your surmising's. 'What if, how do I know, what if there isn't......?' Allow me to challenge you. If there could be such a person who could heal your brokenness, raise you up, empower and restore you so that you are released into your purpose, and arrive at a place where your life becomes a blessing to others; If that person could be identified as none other but God, as the odds were totally against you, wouldn't you be encouraged to believe in the existence of God, and indeed the love of God? 'Is this you?' Perhaps you are at the point of no return. Perhaps this is the next step in your journey of life? Take a moment to think about this challenge. What would be your next steps?

Chapter 7

WHAT IS IN YOUR HAND

Time is money, time is precious. Why sit idly by, when we could be investing our time, and add some value to our lives, and to the lives of others.

Each one of us is born with inherent skills, talents, and gifts. Some of us are even blessed to be what is commonly known as, child prodigies. A child prodigy can be defined as a person who has a skill, talent, or gift, which is so unique not least, because it manifests at such an advance stage, though the person is barely out of nappies!

Do you have access to a pen, a piece of paper, a computer, access to the library and the resources available? Then you have everything you need to start your mission and set your compass to starting you on your new journey. What are your resources? What are your talents/ skills? Remember, if one thing fails, it is not the end. Identify what you have, and the skills and experience you possess, as this is what you are going to rely on. and need, to get you through the dry seasons. Your skills coupled with the wisdom of God, together with his direction, and embracing his supernatural power, will enable you to walk this new road. Do not despise what you have but work it. work it, work it!

Are you one of life's optimists, or do you live in fear and constantly embrace the principles of negativism? Is your glass always half empty, or half full? What is your perspective of life; do you wish for the day to end, or for the day to begin? Do you retire to bed with a feeling of accomplishment, or with the sinking feeling of, if only?

Do you embrace change and challenge, or would you rather stick with what has always been? If you desire change, then you must change your pattern of behaviour; as doing the same thing continuously, whilst hoping for change, will only yield, the same results!

Born again believers (*as illustrated in the book of Acts of the Apostles*) are people of optimism; optimism based on a set of beliefs, followed by appropriate action, and not a whimsical idea or a flight of fancy. Optimism basically means you have hope. You live in hope, and you embrace the principles of hope. Hope ultimately embodies the component of expectation. Optimism says we expect things to be different because we have taken on a new strategy. Or, as that plan of action did not work, we will try another way.

As believers we believe wholly in the concept of hope; the hope of a brighter day, the hope of a new day, the hope of a second chance, the hope that if we fail, we will get up and try again until we succeed.

As believers, we believe that we possess in our hands the ability to do. Our success is dependent upon what we do and how we do it. Releasing the power, or value, of what we have in our hand, will bring success. This concept is best illustrated in the following song which says *"love yields something if you give it away, you end up having more……. it's just like, a magic penny, hold it tight, and you won't have many, lend it, spend it, and you'll have so many, they'll roll all over the floor".*

We must learn how to identify the value of our potential, and the skills and experiences, we have amassed over the years, and invest the same. We can then begin to catch a glimpse of the reality of what we could have, and the possibility or hope of our dream being materialized. We then have what it takes, to turn not only our lives around, but the lives of others, and can also make a positive investment into the lives of others.

Have you ever wondered what makes others good at what they do i.e., being good at their job for example or their vocation? The answer lies in the passion they have for what they do. For passion comes from within, and it is often the driving force which propels us forward and helps us to empower others.

The year 2008 was a year of firsts, the year of new beginnings. Eleven years later. the window of opportunity is still open, and there is still time for those who wish to make their mark, to do so.

2008, as a year of firsts, there were new records to be made as well as new records to be broken. There were also new grounds to cover, and the pioneering of new ideas too.

In the year 2008, there were many Firsts across the spectrum of Nanotechnology, astronomy, general science to medical science, music, public opinion, and changes in politics. We can look at a number of these below:

There is something about being first, a pioneer in the making, a trendsetter, and someone who makes their mark on the global stage. There is, however, something greater, where with the power of influence, you can assist others in empowering themselves, to fill the vacuum in their own lives, and moreover, to impact the lives of others to do what they enjoy doing and are most passionate about. Take for example, the Unitarian person who feels passionate about helping those less fortunate than themselves, through the gift of medicine, and their ability to impact the lives of others for the better. Further, consider, those who go out on missionary trips, and who take sabbaticals to remote countries, like Kabul in Afghanistan. Consider those, who go on mercy missions to impoverished communities, like Haiti after the earthquake in 2012, and those who often put the needs of others before their own. The common thread running through the decisions taken by such people is their passion and the need to assist where they can as it is a cause worth pursing for the general good of everyone else.

It may be lonely being at the top, but you have the enviable position of being a leader; a good leader demonstrating leadership to which others can aspire to.

A First In Astronomy; resulting in the production of the first Photos of Planets around Other Stars. Astronomers have taken what they say are the first-ever direct images of planets outside of our solar system, including a visible-light snapshot of a single-planet system, and an infrared picture of a multiple-planet system. Until now, scientists have inferred the presence of planets, mainly by detecting an unseen world's gravitational tug on its host star or waiting for the planet to transit in front of its star and then detecting a dip in the star's light.

A First In Predicting The Onset Of Earthquakes Scientists achieve a breakthrough in forecasting earthquakes. This was reported in London on June 6. The scientists found a close link between electrical disturbances on the edge of our atmosphere, and impending quakes on the ground below. NASA scientists have said that they could be on the verge of a breakthrough, in their efforts to forecast earthquakes.

According to a report in BBC News, NASA scientists teamed up with experts in the UK to investigate a possible space-based early warning system. All that remains is to find a method of preventing earthquakes.

Cardiff Scientists' Major Breakthrough In Understanding Schizophrenia. People with one of the most stigmatized mental health disorders, were given fresh hope of improved treatment.

A team of scientists from Cardiff University have made a breakthrough in schizophrenia research, by identifying the genes associated with the disease. The discovery is expected to eventually lead to a better understanding of this misunderstood, and feared disease, as well as improved treatments.

On the sweet front, **A Dark Chocolate That Cures What Ails Us.** We know that dark chocolate cocoa powder has up to three times the antioxidants found in green tea, plus twice the antioxidants in red wine; is good for your heart. Studies have shown that dark chocolate's polyphenols affect serotonin levels in the brain; that will boost your mood. But in the year 2008, dark chocolate has gained even more favour in medical circles. In one study, heart-transplant patients showed a decreased risk of clogged arteries two hours after consuming 40 grams of dark chocolate. In another, researchers from the University of Illinois found that subjects who ate a 22-gram Cocoa Via dark chocolate bar daily for two months lowered their blood pressure and cholesterol levels.

On the scientific front a **Major Breakthrough For Dialysis Patients, According To Preliminary Result For Patients Suffering From End-stage Renal Disease** (ESRD). The report showed that a growing number of patients at a Montreal hospital have become the beneficiaries of a North American breakthrough. The benefits are dynamic and include:

1. Improved removal of uremic toxins

2. Decreased number of hospitalizations days

3. A better tolerance for patients

4. Minimizes the state of chronic inflammation, that too often may lead to complications over along course of dialysis and an increased biocompatibility across the blood-dialysis system interface

A First In Genetic Engineering; The UVA Center for Molecular Design and published in the October 29, 2008, issue of *Nature*, revealed the first ever complete structure of a nuclear hormone receptor on human DNA. This is a discovery that now clears a new path for scientists to design more effective drugs with fewer associated health risks. For decades, scientists have been studying nuclear hormone receptors to gain a better understanding of how they turn genes on and off throughout the body and how they function as key drug targets, for several diseases, such as diabetes, breast cancer, osteoporosis, and high cholesterol. Now it looks like their efforts have paid off.

A First In Sport; in November 2008, we witnessed the first Black man ever to win a Formula 1 racing event narrowly beating the Brazilian favourite on his home turf.

A First In Facial Transplants …We witnessed in 2008, the first ever patient to survive a facial transplant, extending the borders of medical science.

Another Medical First…. In 2008 we witnessed the first operation and survival of a conjoined twin, born to the youngest couple ever, to have conjoined twins!

On the musical front **A Major Breakthrough: Music's 'DNA' Decoded**

Peter Neubäcker, the German music software engineer responsible for the popular pitch correction Melodyne, has created a program called Direct Note Access (DNA) that can dissect a chord into individual notes, so that the chord can be re-formed into something new.

For music producers who use computers, which include many of them, this constitutes a major game changer whose implications for the future of music, are deep and widespread. Direct Note Access for example, will make it possible to create an entire album's worth of guitar playing with a single chord, because it can re-form it into any other chord.

In December 2008, the **Wittelsbach Diamond** sold for a record £16.4m, representing the most expensive piece of jewellery, to be sold at auction

Across The Pond in 2008, we witnessed the pre-incumbent inauguration of the first Black president of the United States of America.

What ideas do you have floating around in your head? What will it take for you to act on them and launch out? You never know you could invent or create an idea, that could serve the needs of many, far beyond your own life span.

You could write a book, which would bring inspiration too others, and empower them to reach realms which before, looked impossible.

You do not need to have a degree from Cambridge; (although if you did, this would be an awesome achievement) You do not even require a First-Class honors', (very commendable), or to have gone to law school, or served as a director on a large company, to be positioned to make your mark.

Note, that a pioneer is one who breaks new ground, or whose efforts results in a new record being set. A pioneer is one, who has grafted hard at their task most likely in secret, hidden away in the recesses of their home or office, honing their idea until it is perfect, and ready, to be unleashed on the unsuspecting public. A pioneer is also one, whose idea will benefit everyone with a hope for the future; an idea which certainly does not have as its base, a selfish, self-centered notion, of me, myself, and I.

Chapter 8

WHAT YOU SEE IS WHAT YOU GET

The Lord's command to Noah after the flood had abated, was "to be fruitful, and multiply and replenish the earth". In our day, God would have said now that the famine is over, we have be-come empowered, to impact our generation for good through the wisdom knowledge and skills we have acquired, throughout those years of "lack"

Many of us have may have seen great famine, distress, turbulence, and emotional pain. Now that our experiences have empowered us for the better, it is time to put that experience to work.

We are the Apple of God's eye, and He desires for us to live in the realm of our promise, and inheritance.

To understand the process of restoration and subsequent empowerment, we need to go back to the beginning of creation, to examine the original plan of God for humanity.

God's Seed In Us

When we were conceived in the mind of God, our destiny was also mapped out and pre-determined. The Lord then planted the seed of his concept, within us, The whole sum of our potential is within the seed of His desire for us.

The harvest that God has decreed to us, is in the seed. To illustrate this point, let us look at the apple tree. The whole life span of the apple tree, the kind of apple it will bear i.e., granny smith or golden delicious, for example, the texture of the apple, and the time the tree will blossom, is all embedded in the seed. God plants in us his dream seed for our life, and therefore the harvest we have been praying, for will be in that seed.

What Do We See?

Our notion of God is significant to the fulfillment of our purpose. This picture we see, extends to what we desire, and expect God to be able to do. What we perceive in our minds, is the thing that we create. This is because the process of duplication, multiplication, and empowering, starts in the mind. God uses the experience gained from our past, to build the platform for our future.

There is a season of rest, which is coming to us all. Hard times do not last forever. The struggle we thought would sink us, is **NOT GOING** to signal the end: Rather, it is the **POWER SURGE**, that will bring us to a place of frustration, which ultimately causes us to re-evaluate our plans. our mindset and prepares the platform for our victory parade.

Rome was never built in a day. One does not become a millionaire overnight. The CEO of a major company did not build his empire overnight. For the CEO, who has now reached perhaps the pinnacle of their career, I can almost guarantee, the failures of their past will have helped to steer their path, to enable them to become who, and what, they are today.

God is not biased to any one-person, race or group, but shows favour to whom he will. Why then as children of God do, we think He will not show us his favour? Many times, it is the pattern of our thoughts, that hinder or prevent us, from moving on and progressing forward.

We then run the risk of remaining stuck in a time warp, or a bygone era, looking for others to blame, and being satisfied, that we can at least blame someone else for our failures. But where does that leave us; embittered and powerless to move on! We cannot afford to carry that old pattern of thinking, our failures hurt and pains, into our new day. We need to allow our minds to go through the process of transformation, or metamorphosis, if we are to experience a new day, and a new lease of life. It can, and will, happen as many who have been where we were, and where I once was, will testify.

If we perceive God as incapable of moving a mountain, we remain where we are, the object/s of our desire as a figment of our imagination, forever etched in our mind. 'For as a man thinks in his heart, so he is' (Proverbs 23:7)

No one can hold back that which God has decreed for us. When we sow that seed, whether it is our time, our money, wise counsel, or advice, then this signals to God that we are serious about receiving our harvest. Moreover, that we understand the implications of what will now become expected of us. What would we give to understand God's purpose for us? What would we give to be able to unlock and access God's wealth for us? **BUT**

"Without faith it is impossible to please God for they that come to God must believe that he is God and that he is a believer of them that diligently seek him" (Hebrews 11:6)

Keys To Building A Platform For The Future

1.   Free Yourself

You need to free yourself by freeing and forgiving those who you believe, correctly or incorrectly, have hurt or harmed you. Many of the people who you hold accountable for your current position in life, do not even know that you are blaming them. Instead, these people, are living delivered, and prosperous lives. You, however, remain the same, still hurting. The fact is if you free your enemies, you will free yourself. **The knowledge of the truth then makes you accountable for what you do or fail, to do, i.e., the act of commission, or omission.**

2. Slay The Demon Of Apathy

Say good-bye to **APATHY**. Doing nothing helps no one. Taking stock of where you are, and where you want to be, requires action. Act today.

3. Focus On How To Make A Difference

Once you have discovered purpose, and are empowered, you will then begin to understand that your talents and abilities, can be of service to others.

4. Embrace Your Values

Your passion aspirations and values are often indicative of your purpose and will motivate you to empower others to find their place and position, in the earth.

5. Act ON PURPOSE

Dream it and then do it

Think! I think therefore I am

Because I can think it, I am therefore able to do it

6.   Be Purposeful In All Domains

Understand your purpose. Deal with the gaps and those parts of your life lacking expression.

7.   Encourage Others To Find Purpose.

This is a powerful tool. Once you have been empowered and motivated by the discovery of your purpose, you will want to tell your friends, and neighbours primarily, because you have discovered the meaning to life. and cannot imagine living life any other way.

8   Learn From Failure

Failure should be regarded as stepping-stones on your route to success and your desired goals in life. The truest test of your character as a leader, is the way you deal with failure.

9.   Be Flexible

Try not to adopt a rigid timetable. You may have to make many attempts at succeeding before you receive your crown.

Bibliography

1. Articles referred to in Chapter 7 sourced from The Associated Press News 2008
2. How does a caterpillar turn into a butterfly – "discover wildlife.com"

Make Your Own Notes

Make Your Own Notes

Make Your Own Notes

Make Your Own Notes

Make Your Own Notes

Printed in Great Britain
by Amazon

81082976R00068